Family Faith TALKS

100 Discipleship Activities and Conversation Starters

SANDY ATWOOD

randall house

114 Bush Rd | Nashville, TN 37217
randallhouse.com

To William and Lydia -
my grands!
May they always
love God.

Table Of Contents

Introduction

Introduction

Do you ever feel as if you can't do one more thing? You are already juggling work, kids' school and activities, church, housework, meals, shopping, cleaning . . . and the list goes on. Now here's a book about adding spiritual conversations to your days! I get it. I am a mom of four (now grown), but I remember days when I was hanging on by a thread—a very frayed thread.

If you are like me, you want to have meaningful conversations with your kids. I'm not here to make you feel guilty (we are already pretty good at doing that to ourselves!), but I want to encourage and help you. When someone mentions spiritual conversations or devotions, we think we have to line up everyone on the sofa and make all the kids sit still and listen. (*I know I lost you at "sit still!"*) What if there is a better way? Deuteronomy 6:5-7 says, "And you must love the LORD your God with all your heart, all your soul, and all your strength. And you must commit yourselves wholeheartedly to these commands that I am giving you today. Repeat them again and again to your children. *[That part I've got!]* Talk about them when you are at home and when you are on the road, when you are going to bed and when you are getting up." (NLT)

What if we look for ways to talk about God throughout the day? What if, while you're putting on a BAND-AID®, you talk about compassion for others? What if your child is afraid and you share a time when you were afraid and God helped you? What if you talk about making good choices while you're in the car, using a stoplight as a visual illustration?

I've compiled lots of ideas to help you include God in your everyday activities. As we love God (that is the place to start), we can share Him with our families. If we never talk about Him, maybe our kids will get the idea that He's not all that important. This book gives you lots of ways to talk about God—there are game ideas, questions to ask, Bible verses to read, and prayers to pray. Read through the book and find an idea you like and try it on your family. See what they think. Most don't require any other items (except for a few science or cooking experiments). You might be surprised at how eager your kids are to learn from you!

A bit of instruction on how to conduct each activity: the statements in bold are what I recommend you say to your family. So begin today having conversations that lead to discipleship in your home.

Blessings,

Sandy

Authority

1. Rules Are Good

Play a game of kickball to see the need for authority and rules. Divide the kids into two teams. Set up the bases and home plate. Flip a coin to see who goes first. Tell them the rules:

1. Three kicks (tries) and you are out.
2. If you are tagged by the ball, you are out.
3. When you run around three bases and then home, you score a run.

*Depending on the ages of your kids, you may need to adjust rules or game. The idea can work with any game.

Announce that you will be the referee and scorekeeper. Allow them to play a couple of minutes keeping score, but then change the rules. (Call someone out after only two kicks/tries. Announce someone is safe even after being tagged by the ball. Declare a home run after a person gets to first base. Call the ball out of bounds when it really was not. Give three points for a run.)

End the game and talk about it:

How did you feel when I kept changing the rules?

Why is it important that we have an authority who makes good rules and enforces them?

Everyone is happier and enjoys it more when we know and keep the rules. Games (and life) are chaotic when there is no authority to make or enforce the rules. Rules make games fair and better.

2. You Said WHAT?

Can you say something without any words?

Pantomime (no words) the different attitudes we might have toward those in authority. Write the words *respectful* and *disrespectful* on an index card or piece of paper. (Place these face down so kids cannot see the words.) Share a situation and ask for two volunteers who will choose a card and then act out a possible response, per the card they chose.

Some situations to get you thinking: (I am sure you can think of some that apply to your house!)
- Parent says, "Turn off the TV!"
- Teacher gives extra homework.
- Coach sends you to the bench.
- Pastor says, "God wants us to forgive others."
- Mom says, "No snack before dinner."
- Dad says, "Pick up the trash in the yard."
- School bus driver tells everyone to be quiet.
- Teacher says, "Today we are going to play a get-to-know-you game."

Read Hebrews 13:7 and ask: *Why should we obey those in authority over us?* (They are keeping watch over you; they will have to give an account; hopefully they are wise and want what is best for you, etc.)

We are to respect those in authority. We can "say" a lot about respect/disrespect without saying a word! We can still be respectful even when we disagree.

3. Rules, Rules, Rules!

At the dinner table or while driving, ask kids about rules:

- *Are rules good or bad?*
- *What is the worst rule you can think of?*
- *What might happen if there were NO rules?*
- *Why do we have rules?*
- *Think of the rule you most dislike. Why don't you like it? Is there a reason it should be obeyed?*

Rules are for our good. They help us know the right thing to do. Obeying the rules can protect us and help us get along with others.

Make a short list of family rules and post them on the fridge. Knowing what is expected makes it easier to obey.

4. Practice

Write each of the following reactions on a slip of paper and put them in a basket. (If you have older kids, you might not even need the prompts; they can think of the different responses themselves.)

- pout
- get mad and stomp foot
- argue that your job is too hard
- say you will obey, but get busy and forget to do it
- whine
- complain about what others are doing
- say mean things about the person telling you to obey
- say, "Sure, I will do it"
- smile
- listen carefully to what you are being told to do
- encourage others by offering to help
- do it right away
- politely ask for help if you need it

Different people respond differently when told to do something by parents or others in authority. Take turns letting family members draw a slip of paper and act out the different responses. After each one is acted out, let the others guess the response and decide if it is the right/wrong way to respond to authority.

Read Titus 3:1-2.

What should be our attitude toward authority? (Be submissive; be obedient; be ready for every good work; speak no evil; do not quarrel.)

It is important to submit to/obey those who are in charge of us, but it is also important to do it with a right attitude.

Choices

5. You Pick

Put a kitchen utensil (fork, spoon, knife, straw, toothpick, giant serving spoon, spatula, etc.) in a bag (one per bag—make sure the bag conceals the utensil) and close the bag. Invite each family member to choose his or her eating utensil for dinner from the bags (no touching to see what might be inside either). Each person must eat dinner using ONLY the utensil he or she chose. (Hopefully, there will be some laughter!)

What would have made your choice easier? (Being able to see what was in the bags.)

What are some choices we make each day? (What cereal to eat; what clothes to wear; what game to play; whether to yell at a sibling or speak kind words; whether to tell the truth or a lie; and lots more!)

Read Proverbs 3:5-6. *What does this verse tell us about making choices?* (Do not lean to just what you want; acknowledge God; trust in Him to lead you; go God's way; etc.)

God gives us a free will to choose. Choosing His way (as told to us in the Bible) is the best way.

6. Two Choices

Stand in the middle of the room and tell the kids you will give them two choices. They will go and stand on either side of the room to indicate their choices. (If you like _____, go to the left side [pointing to the left]. If you like _____, go to the right side [pointing to the right].) Add some choices particular to your family, if you like.

Choices:

- pepperoni or cheese pizza
- chocolate or vanilla ice cream
- playing video games or board games
- riding your bike or cleaning your room
- vacation at the beach or the mountains
- singing or drawing
- math or history
- dogs or cats
- soccer or baseball

Say something like this:

Some choices in life do not really matter—like if you eat chocolate or vanilla ice cream. Many choices do matter. God made us and knows what is best for us. *Where can we find God's way and wisdom?* (In the Bible.) **Proverbs is a book in the Bible written by Solomon, the wisest man who ever lived.**

Read some Proverbs about wisdom and then ask, *"What can you learn about making wise choices from this verse?"* (Some good ones are Proverbs 1:5; 14:16; 15:20; 17:28; and 21:20.)

7. Red, Yellow, Green

When driving, use the stoplight to teach kids how to make decisions.

- *STOP and THINK (RED)*
- *CAUTIOUSLY Consider the Choices (YELLOW)*
- *GO GOD'S WAY (GREEN)*

STOP and THINK (RED)

Why is it good to stop and think before making a choice? (It keeps you from just following the crowd; keeps you from reacting wrongly; etc.)

A wise person doesn't just follow the crowd. A wise person doesn't just do what he feels like doing. He stops and thinks before he does things. If we would only stop and think before we say or do anything, we might keep ourselves from saying or doing something wrong.

CAUTION, Consider the Choices (YELLOW)

Two questions to ask:

1. *Does the Bible say anything about this?*
   Not all choices are equal. Some are between right and wrong; some are between wise and unwise things.

   If the Bible has specifically said something is wrong, we should choose NOT to say or do it. But not all choices are between right and wrong. How do you decide when you have a choice between two okay things?

2. *What is the WISE thing to do?*

GO GOD'S WAY (GREEN)

Choosing to GO GOD'S WAY is always best. If something is clearly wrong, then the wisest choice would be to say no or walk away. If something is not wrong and it would be wise to do it . . . then do it! We want to daily choose to follow God's way and rules.

Give the kids some chances to practice making choices using the stoplight.

Some situations: your friend asks you to steal something; a friend wants you to disobey your parents; you want to eat cookies just before dinner; you want to play your video game but have homework; you have an hour of free time; etc.

8. Which Way?

Take a walk (or drive) with your kids. Every time you come to an intersection, flip a coin—heads, go left; tails, go right. See where you end up.

Ask:

Is this a good way to make decisions? It might be a fun way to pick when you do not care where you end up, but it is a good idea to know where you are going, especially when making a choice about right and wrong. *What if we flipped a coin to decide whether we should tell a lie or obey a parent?* Not a good idea!

The Bible tells us that if we go our own way, it might lead us into a wrong path.

Read Proverbs 14:12. **There is a way that seems right to us, but in the end it leads to death. That is why we need to follow Jesus. He said, "I am the way, the truth, and the life"** (John 14:6). **When we read and follow His words in the Bible, we will know how to go to Heaven and how to live while we are on earth. Following Jesus always leads us the right way!**

9. Which One?

While waiting somewhere, play rock school (a game I often played as a little girl and played with my own kids while we were waiting). All you need is a small rock (or penny). Start everyone at the same place side by side (this is kindergarten). Put the rock in one hand (behind your back so they cannot see which hand you put it in) and let each kid guess (one at a time) which hand has the rock in it. If they guess correctly, they move to the "next grade"; if they guess the wrong hand, they stay where they are until their next turn to guess. The first one to "twelfth grade" is the winner.

Would it have been easier to pick the hand with the rock if you could have seen both hands open before you made a choice? Of course! *Does it help you to make a better choice if you know what is right?* (Hopefully!)

Read Proverbs 1:5. **Listening to the people in charge (parents!) can help you make right choices. Reading the Bible to find out what God wants will help you make right choices. Knowing the consequences before making a choice can sometimes help us make a better choice. If I know it will hurt my friend's feelings if I say mean words, I can choose to keep my mouth shut and not say them. Our choices affect others and we want to make good choices.**

10. Domino!

Stand up a row of dominos (just far enough apart so that they will all fall down when the first one is tapped). Tap the first domino and see what happens.

Optional Idea: If you do not have dominos, you could build a tower with blocks. After building the tower, ask one of the kids to pull out one of the lower blocks. (The tower should come tumbling down.) Do it again.

After doing this several times, ask:

What happened when we tapped the first domino (or what happened when we pulled out the block)? (The whole thing fell down.)

One thing caused another. There are results when we do certain things. Sometimes we call these results consequences.

Tell or read the story of Adam and Eve's sin from Genesis 3. ***What were the results of Adam and Eve's sin?*** (They hid from God instead of wanting to see Him; they had to leave the Garden of Eden; they were punished by God; etc.)

What happens when we sin? (Bad things happen—now or later.) ***What are some consequences when we sin?*** (We feel guilty. We may be punished. Others may not trust us if we lie to them.) **Sin (breaking God's rules) is a terrible thing, and there will always be bad results when we sin.**

*Consequences are not always seen right away, but even if we do not get caught there is the tendency to think we can get away with sin, and that is definitely a bad consequence.

11. What to Do If

Ask your kids:

Will you always make right choices? (Unfortunately, no!)

What should you do when you make a wrong choice?

Read 1 John 1:9 aloud. ***What does this tell us we should do when we make a wrong choice and sin?*** **Confess and tell God we sinned and ask Him to forgive us. He is merciful and will forgive our sins and take them all away.**

Parents, you may want to share what you do when you make a wrong choice. When they hear you asking God for forgiveness, they will begin to understand God's grace.

When our wrong choices involve hurting other people, we need to tell others that we are sorry. When parents make a wrong choice, it is good to say, "I am sorry I yelled at you. I am sorry I lied."

Jesus is bigger than our wrong choices. He forgives us and still loves us even when we fail to make right choices.

Contentment

12. Which Is Better?

Ask your kids to compare two items (two vegetables, two fruits, two cookies, whatever you like). *What do you like about each one? What don't you like? Why? Do you like one better than the other? What makes you like one more?*

Comparing one vegetable to another is not bad, but what does the Bible say about comparing ourselves to others? Read 2 Corinthians 10:12. **It is not wise to compare.**

What can happen when we compare ourselves to others? (We can feel bad when we think we cannot do something as well as they can; we can feel proud when we can do something better than they can; etc.)

In the Bible, when people were praising David for his bravery and skill in defeating Goliath, King Saul was angry and eventually tried to kill David because he was jealous of him (1 Samuel 18:6-9).

What are some statements a jealous person might think or say?

- Others should be praising me.
- He/she has it better than me.
- They like him/her more than me.
- I want bad things to happen to that person.

Instead of feeling sad or mad, what can we think or say? (I am glad they were able to get that; I have lots of toys already; I am happy with what I have; they have different abilities than I do; etc.)

We usually feel jealous when we compare ourselves to others.

13. That's Not Fair

To introduce the topic of jealousy, open a snack that your kids will like and pass out some to each child. Give all a fair amount but make sure that one gets quite a bit more than the others. (They will quickly point out that someone else got more or say, "That's not fair.")

Why weren't you happy with the snack I gave you? (You gave him more; I want more; I did not get enough; etc.)

Why did you feel bad/sad when your sibling received more than you did? **There is a name for that feeling and it is called jealousy.**

What is jealousy? (Bad feelings—anger, bitterness, or even hatred toward someone for having something we want.)

Life is not always fair and sometimes others receive something that we do not. Comparing what you have with what others have is not good. You can never know what God is doing in someone else's life. He is a loving God and He will give you what is best for you. He is kind and generous.

14. Be Content

We all feel jealous at times, but the answer for jealousy is to BE CONTENT! Instead of focusing on what we DO NOT have or what we CANNOT do, we should focus on what we DO have and what we CAN do.

Every time you are tempted to be jealous, make a list (either on paper or in your mind) of a couple of things you have or can do. Brainstorm some things that we could think or say when we feel jealous in each of the following situations.

- *The coach praised your teammate for a great hit but did not say anything when you made a great hit.*
- *Your older sibling gets to stay up later than you.*
- *The teacher let the other group go out to recess earlier than your group.*
- *You think your friend is prettier than you.*
- *Your best friend got the game you have been wanting for months.*

Be content with what you have and what you can do.

15. What About Him?

Gather everyone around the table and pass out paper and pencils/crayons. Instruct kids to draw a picture . . . while looking at the person's picture on their right (to illustrate the idea that looking at others is often why we are not happy with our lives).

What was hard about drawing your picture? (I could not pay attention and enjoy drawing my picture because I was looking at theirs.)

Why is it easy to be envious when we look at what others have or what good things happen to them? (We cannot appreciate what we have because we are looking at and wishing we could have what others have; someone has something better or newer or cooler, etc.)

Read Proverbs 14:30. **Envy is like a rottenness in the bones. When we are content with what we have, we will not need to envy what others have.**

16. You Can't Steal My Joy

Play a game to talk about contentment and joy. Give each person a sheet of paper and a pen or marker. Ask them to think of things that take away/steal their joy. Another way to say that is to name things that make you unhappy or not satisfied. Here are some suggestions:

- *My bike is old and not very good.*
- *I wish I had what _____ has.*
- *I never get to be first.*
- *I had to do an extra chore.*
- *My teacher gave too much homework.*
- *I am afraid of a storm.*
- *I am worried about my spelling test.*

Tape the piece of paper (which has a "joy-stealing statement" on it) to each one's back. Write "JOY" on one piece of paper and choose one person to have joy and tape the "JOY" page on his back. The object of the game is for the joy stealers to grab the "JOY" sign.

Play this game in a large, open area—outside if possible. Mark an area of safety with masking tape on one end where the person with joy can go. Line all the joy stealers up at one end of the field or room and at the signal of "go," they must chase the person with the "JOY" sign and try to steal it. Any time the person with joy runs behind the safety line, the joy stealers cannot steal it.

When someone steals the joy, play stops and a new person gets the joy sign and play resumes with the "joy stealers" trying to grab the "JOY" from the new person.

After a few rounds, rest and talk about it:

- *Does it ever seem like people or events keep stealing your joy? If so, how?*
- *What is joy?*
- *How can you get it?*
- *Which is easier: to get it or lose it?*

Philippians 4:4 tells us to have JOY always!

How can we be glad even when things are not like we want? **Not everything that happens is good and we do not have to like it, but we can be glad because God is with us and will help us** (Psalm 16:11).

17. How Much?

Elisabeth Elliot was a missionary to Ecuador. When she and her young daughter, Valerie, went to live among the Auca Indians to try and reach them for Christ, they took only what they could carry on their backs (a cooking pot, two bowls, two forks, etc.). And she said that still the Indians asked, "Why do you have so much?"

Ask your kids:

If you went to live in another culture and could take only what you could carry in your backpack, what would YOU take?

What do you really NEED to live? What does 1 Timothy 6:8 tell us we need?
(Food and clothing.)

We can choose to be content, no matter how much or how little we have.

Optional: Send them to their rooms to count how many toys they have and report back.

18. Ouch!

When putting a BAND-AID® on your child, talk about compassion.

Why do we need BAND-AIDS®? (We have been hurt.)

When you are hurt, what would you like for someone to do for you? (Help you; say kind words; get help if needed; be gentle, etc.)

What are some things that do not help when you are hurt? (Telling you what you did wrong; being harsh; ignoring you; talking about themselves, etc.)

Not all our hurts are physical; sometimes our hurt can be emotional. We can feel lonely when we are left out of a game. We can feel sad when a good friend moves away. We can feel hurt when someone says mean words. We can feel hurt in many ways. We all need caring and kindness.

Ephesians 2:4 says God is RICH in mercy. Mercy is giving people kindness even though they may not deserve it. *How does God treat us when we are hurting?* Even when we do wrong things, God is quick to forgive and help us. We can be like Him and show compassion to others.

19. Walk a Mile in My Shoes

Put everyone's shoes in a pile in the middle of the room. At a signal to go, see how quickly everyone can grab a matching pair of shoes (not their own), put them on, and be the first to walk to a designated spot. (Little ones may need additional help.)

Ask:

Have you ever heard the saying, "Walk a mile in my shoes"?

What does it mean? (Do not criticize someone until you have walked/lived in their situation; we do not know how someone feels if we have not been in their circumstance; etc.)

How can we comfort others who are suffering? (With kind words; with loving actions; think of what has helped you and do that for them.)

What would you want someone to do if:

- you fall down and scrape your knee
- you are sick in bed
- your best friend moves away
- your grandma is in the hospital
- your dog dies
- you make a bad grade
- you are lonely

Read 2 Corinthians 1:3-4. **God is called the God of all comfort. He comforts us in our trouble so we can learn to comfort others who are suffering. If you have felt lonely and someone befriended you, you will know how to be a friend to someone else who needs a friend. We all need compassion, not criticism. We cannot always know how or what another person feels, but we treat the other person like we would want to be treated. We can show kindness and try to help.**

20. Act Like You Love One Another

Get the creative juices going and make puppets out of whatever materials you have on hand (sock singles, popsicle sticks, markers, scraps of fabric, yarn, etc.). After each person makes a puppet, act out some scenarios (with the puppets) of when and how to show compassion. Pair up two or more, give them an idea, and let them think of and perform a short show.

Some ideas:

- A new girl feels left out on the playground.
- A sibling wants to play a game.
- Mom is cooking dinner and the baby is crying.
- A neighbor breaks your toy.
- Your good friend is sick.

Clap loudly for each show!

Read Matthew 7:12. *According to this verse, how should we treat others?* (We should treat them as we would want to be treated.) **This verse is called the Golden Rule. Another way we say it is: Do unto others as you would have them do unto you.**

21. Ah! You Cared

Grab the art supplies (construction or white paper, markers, crayons, pencils, stickers, glitter, etc.) and make a card for someone who might be suffering (in the hospital, alone, sick at home, mourning a loss, etc.) and might need some encouraging words.

Draw a picture and write words that could help. (I am sorry you are sick. Feel better soon. God loves you. I am praying for you. God hears you.) Ask older kids to help the younger ones write their kind messages. Mail or deliver the cards.

22. Sharing Is Caring

Make a small badge out of construction paper or cardstock that says, *Share Award*. Announce that one family member will win the *Share Award* each day.

Look for examples of sharing during the day and point them out. "Thanks for sharing your popcorn with me." "Seth let Gabe play with his cars this afternoon." "Anna, that is kind of you to let your sister play with your art supplies."

Announce the winner of the *Share Award* every evening at dinner and reward him/her with a special privilege: stay up 30 minutes late, choose a game to play, pick a snack, choose an extra book to read, etc. (Praise is a good way to reinforce the behavior we want to see more.)

God has given us so much that we want to share with others.

23. Do Good . . . to All

Galatians 6:10 says that whenever we have the opportunity, we should do good to everyone, especially to those in the family of faith.

What are some ways we can do good? (help with a chore; play a game together; write a thank you to someone; listen; say kind words; think of ways to make what someone does easier; etc.)

Give each family member a few Post-It® notes. Walk to different locations inside and outside the house and ask the question: ***How could you "do good" to someone in this location?*** Allow those with an idea to write it on their Post-It® note and stick it there. (There should be lots of ideas all over the house: help with the dishes, take out the trash, put away the toys, give a foot rub, read a book to a sibling, etc.)

Ask each family member to choose one way or more from all the ideas posted and do good. When they do the good deed, they can stick the Post-It® note on the fridge (or other designated place). See how long it takes to do the good deeds and collect all the notes.

 **Love is . . .**

Make a memory game with characteristics of love from 1 Corinthians 13. If you have older kids, ask them to look up the chapter and find the characteristics. Write each characteristic on two Post-It® notes with a pencil (a marker will show through). (If the note is only sticky on one side, be sure to write on the back.)

Characteristics of love:

- Patient
- Kind
- Happy when truth wins
- Never gives up
- Never loses faith
- Always hopeful
- Endures through every situation

Then write some of the characteristics (twice) that love is NOT:

- NOT Jealous
- NOT Proud
- NOT Rude
- NOT Demanding
- NOT Irritable

Mix up the Post-It® notes and stick them face down. Take turns turning over two at a time. If they are the same (a match), the person finding them gets to keep the match until the end of the game. After all matches have been found, sort them in two categories: what love is and what love is NOT.

 **Love Signal**

The best place to start loving is at home! Think of a "secret" signal that means "I love you." How about squeezing the other person's hand three times? How about tapping your heart? How about linking your two index fingers together? Practice the signal and see which one gives the signal to the other family member first, especially out in public.

Courage

26. Where Can I Get Some Courage?

Brainstorm situations where one might feel afraid and act out ways to get courage. Write each situation (some are given below) on a slip of paper and put them in a bag or hat.

- You want to sleep at a friend's house, but you are afraid.
- You want to tell your friends about Jesus, but you are afraid they might laugh at you.
- You see your younger sister being bullied.
- You are afraid of storms.
- You want to be in the school play, but you are afraid to get up in front of others.
- You want to tell the truth, but you are afraid of getting in trouble.
- Your best friend wants to cheat off your paper.

Take turns drawing a slip of paper and offering solutions (with words or by acting it out).

Read Psalm 46:1-3. **King David (who wrote many psalms) said that God was his refuge, a place where he could go to feel safe. God was with David, and David depended on God for help.**

Memorize Psalm 46:1. Write each word of the Bible verse on an index card or piece of paper. Place these in order along the way (taped to a mailbox, tree, fence, etc., or strategically placed on a bush, car, or wherever) for kids to collect as you take a walk.

Say the first word when you find it; say the first then second word together when you find it; say the first, second, and third words in order when you find the third word, etc. Hopefully, you will learn it well if you say it from the beginning each time you find a new word. Remind your kids to say this verse when afraid.

We do not have to be afraid wherever we are, because God is our refuge and makes us strong!

27. Comfort

At bedtime, ask your child:

What gives you comfort? (A special blanket or stuffed animal?)
How would you feel if you could not find it or if it was taken away?
When do you need comfort?

Say something like this:

It makes you feel good to have a special blanket or stuffed animal when you go to bed, doesn't it? It probably even makes you feel comforted knowing it is in your room, if you should need it. Even though we may face hard situations where we are afraid, God gives us some words to comfort us.

Open the Bible and let your child read Hebrews 13:5b-6 ("I will never leave you"). Remind your child that these are God's words written to him. Let your child repeat the phrase, "I will never leave you." Hold up a different finger as you say each word and then place the child's hand over his heart. Let your child repeat this phrase several times and encourage him to say it whenever he needs comfort.

What has God promised? ("I will never leave you.") **We can have courage because God is with us!** Say a prayer thanking God that He is with us and will help us.

28. Afraid of What?!

Make a list of the "Top 10 Things that Make You Afraid." Invite kids to add to the list things that can make us feel afraid (possibly first day of school, spending the night away from home, a bad storm, facing a bully, getting lost from a parent, standing for what is right, fear of being made fun of).

We all feel afraid. We may not try new things or even do what is right because we are too afraid of failing or afraid of what others may think. We all need courage!

What is courage? (doing the right thing, even when we feel afraid)

Will you be afraid if you have courage? (True courage does the right thing WHILE we are still afraid.)

Read the story of Gideon in Judges 6:11-14. Gideon was hiding when the angel visited him.

Why was Gideon afraid? (The Midianites were raiding their towns and stealing their food; they were oppressing the people; etc.) *What did the angel tell Gideon?* **The Lord is with you!**

Do you think Gideon was afraid when he went to battle with the Midianites? **Probably, but he obeyed God and won a victory for Israel and defeated the Midianites** (Judges 7:17-22).

How can you get this courage?

- **Remember this: God is with you.**
- **Ask Him to help you when you feel afraid.**
- **Ask Him to show you what to do.**
- **Ask Him to make you strong inside to do what you should do.**

29. See What God Did!

Gather art supplies and invite family members to think of a time when God helped them and illustrate it. If they draw a blank, ask some questions:

- *When did you feel afraid and God gave you courage?*
- *Has God answered a prayer?*
- *Did God send someone to comfort you when you were sad or lonely?*
- *Is there a Bible verse that helped you know what to do?*

Write this important message across the top or bottom of the picture: **God is with me!** Post their sign where they will see it every day as a reminder of God's presence in your home.

30. Replace It

Teach your kids the "replace it" principle. Instead of just saying, "Don't think about it, don't be afraid," **REPLACE** those fearful thoughts with faith-filled thoughts from the Bible (Romans 10:17).

Ask each family member to think of a situation where one might feel afraid and write it on a slip of paper or index card. Put the slips in a jar or bowl and take turns drawing out a slip. Then think of true statements about God **(God is with me; God loves me; God is for me; God wants to help me; God has all power; etc.)** or find an actual Bible verse that would build trust in God in that situation (some examples might include Joshua 1:9; Psalm 23; Psalm 56:3-4; Isaiah 41:10; Ephesians 6:10).

Write the faith statements on slips of paper. Rip up the fearful thoughts and place the faith-filled thoughts in the jar so they can be pulled out and read when needed.

*A good website to help you find verses is www.biblegateway.com. You can type in a word, and it will bring up all the verses with that word in it.

Encouragement/ Helping Others

31. Helpful Words

Gather everyone in a circle. Announce that whoever you throw the ball to will be "it" and will move to the center of the circle. Then everyone else will think of one kind statement to say about that person. (You help me pick up my toys. You let me share your game. You are funny. You can run fast.) Continue letting others be "it" and sharing until all have had a turn to be encouraged.

How did you feel when others were saying kind words about you?

Why is it so important to say words that help others? (We all get discouraged; kind words can help us keep going; etc.)

Read Ephesians 4:29-32. *What kind of words should we say?* (Words that help and build up others; kind words; not angry or mean words; etc.)

We all need encouragement!

 **32.** You Can Do It

Items needed: paper cups, bucket of water, empty bowl or pitcher, timer
Optional: a whistle for the referees and a pompom for the cheerleaders

Run a relay to fill an empty pitcher with water from the bucket one cup at a time. Choose two people in the family to be the referees (discouragers—pointing out all the mistakes) and the cheerleaders (encouragers—giving words that help). Run the relay twice. The first time, have the referees point out the mistakes (you will never make it; you dropped some water; you are too slow; etc.). Then run it a second time with the cheerleaders giving words of encouragement (you can do it; you are almost there; you are going to win; etc.). Time them to see how quickly they can do it.

When finished, ask:

How did you feel when others were shouting discouraging words to you?

How did you feel when they were shouting encouragement?

What words of encouragement did they shout to you?

Did their encouragement make you want to keep going?

Read 1 Thessalonians 5:11. *What are we to do with our words?* (Encourage and build up one another.)

We need to speak words that encourage/build up others—not words that tear down.

 **33.** Kind Words

Give each family member a blank bookmark (card stock or construction paper cut into bookmark-sized pieces) and a pencil or pen. Each person should write his or her name at the top of a bookmark. Pass each bookmark to the person to the right who will write a kind word that describes the person whose name is on the top of the bookmark. Continue passing the bookmark until it arrives back to the owner. (You may need to help younger ones write their word.)

Ask each person to read his or her encouraging words aloud. Keep the bookmark and read it often.

Faith

34. Faith in What?

Rustle everyone to the dining room and climb up on the table. Tell them that the table is going to take all of you to the ice cream store (depending on the ages of your kids, you can pretend to start it as you would a car).

Could this table drive us to the store? (No matter how much you believed that the table could drive you to the store, it cannot!)

Then gather everyone in the car and tell them the car is going to take you to the ice cream store (or wherever you choose).

Could this car get us to the store? Yes. *Why?* It has done so in the past. It has proven that it is reliable and able to make it to the store.

Drive to the store and enjoy a treat. Talk about it.

Does it matter what you place your faith in? **Yes! No matter how much we believed that the table could get us to the store, it could not. We must put our faith in the right place.** *In whom should we put our faith?*

Read Deuteronomy 4:35, 39. **There is one true God, the God who created the world. The God who rules in Heaven. The God who sent His Son Jesus to the earth. It is not enough to have faith; we must put our faith in a reliable source: GOD!**

35. Invisible

Do a simple experiment to show that things exist (air), even though we cannot see them. Take an empty water or soda bottle and lay it horizontally on a table. Carefully set a small wadded up ball of paper towel in the mouth of the bottle. (The ball should be about half the size of the opening.) Challenge kids to blow the ball of paper into the bottle.

After several tries, ask, *Why is this so impossible?* **The bottle is already filled with air. You are trying to force more air into the bottle, but there is nowhere for the air already inside to go except back out the mouth of the bottle, taking the paper ball with it.**

Can you see air? **No, but you can see the effects of air through the leaves blowing and limbs swaying.**

Can you see God? **No, but we can see the things He has made and see that He is at work in the world, answering prayers and helping people.**

Read Hebrews 11:6. *What is faith?* **Faith is believing in God, although we cannot see Him. We believe there is one true God who made the world and everything in it. We believe He loves us and wants to have a friendship with us.**

What are some ways we can know about God? (We can look at creation and see that since there is a world, there must be a world maker; we can read in the Bible about Him and the miracles He did; we can talk to Him and He will answer our prayers; we can ask forgiveness and know that He will save us; etc.)

36. Eyewitness

Share an object lesson about being a witness.

What is a witness? (Someone who tells what they know or what they have seen.)

To illustrate what a witness is, ask a family member to act out a simple scene. (Give a dollar bill to the volunteer.)

What did you just witness? (Wait for responses.) **You are all witnesses to what happened. I gave the dollar bill to _____. A witness tells what he or she saw and knows. You told me what you saw.**

Thank the volunteer and ask if you can borrow his or her dollar bill for a minute. Show the dollar bill. *Whose picture is on the front?* If you guessed George Washington's picture, you are right. *Who is George Washington?* (First President.) *Were you alive when George Washington was President?* No. *How do we know he was the first President?* We know George Washington was the first President because eyewitnesses saw him and recorded what he did and said in a book.

The resurrection of Jesus is a historical event. Eyewitnesses saw Jesus alive after He died on the cross. The disciples met with Jesus many times after He came back to life. In fact, over 500 people saw Jesus alive after His resurrection (1 Corinthians 15:6). **The Gospels (Matthew, Mark, Luke, and John) were eyewitness accounts, and they give a record of what Jesus said and did. We believe in the Resurrection because this historical account is true.**

37. Guess Who?

Long before Jesus came to earth as a baby, God promised to send One who would deliver all people from sin and gave the people many clues so they would recognize Him.

Invite a special guest (family, friend, or neighbor) to drop by your house at a specific time in the evening. Tell the kids at breakfast about the special guest, but do not reveal his/her identity. Give them clues about the person throughout the day, starting with general ones and ending with more specific. (It is a person. It is a man. He has two eyes. He wears glasses. He is tall. He has gray hair. He is kind. He will play a game with you. Choose your clues to fit the person.)

When the person arrives, ask:

Did the clues help you figure out our guest's identity? Why or why not? (They helped us to recognize him when we saw him.)

How did God give clues to the people BEFORE He sent Jesus to the earth? (The prophets gave many facts/clues about Jesus: where He would be born, who would be His mother, what He would do when He grew up, etc.)

Read Isaiah 61:1-2. *What are some clues about Jesus and the things He would do?* (Preach the good news to the poor; bind up the broken hearted; etc.) **This was written hundreds of years before His birth. Many other prophecies were given before Jesus came to earth and He fulfilled them. God wanted the people to recognize Jesus when He came to earth, but many did not. He gives us reasons to believe in Jesus. Faith is believing in Jesus even though we have not seen Him. We may not have seen Jesus, but people who** were eyewitnesses wrote their experiences in the Bible so we could know what He is like and what He did. Yes, we still have to have faith, but it is a faith built on facts and truth.

*Fulfilled prophecy is one good way to know the Bible is true. Some scholars believe there are over 300 references in the Old Testament that were fulfilled in Jesus. Prophets wrote about His birth, life, and death hundreds of years before He came to earth. This should give us confidence in the accuracy and truth of the Bible (2 Peter 1:19-21).

38. Trust Me

A simple test can help your kids understand a little about faith. If your children are younger, place them on a porch or steps and ask:

Do you think I am strong enough to catch you? Reassure them that you will catch them. Let them jump into your arms and give them a big hug. Do this several times.

Say something like this: **You jumped because you believed I would catch you. You did not know for sure, but you had faith that I would do what I said. God is strong and powerful. God wants us to trust Him and to believe that He will do what He has said. We can always count on God to keep His word.**

39. Reliable Faith

Grab a couple of chairs (one very sturdy and one broken or wobbly) for an object lesson.

(If you do not have a broken chair, ask kids to imagine one. Adapt any ideas if you do not have everything that is mentioned.)

Show both chairs and ask:

Which chair would you like to sit in? Why?

Which chair best represents our faith in God?

Some people think that our faith in God is like sitting in the broken chair. We try it (believing in Him) and *hope* that it holds us. But God is like a sturdy chair—completely reliable. Millions of people have believed in God throughout history and have proved Him to be trustworthy. (Ask a kid to sit in the chair.) Read parts of Hebrews 11 to hear of many different people who completely trusted God.

Ask a kid to hover just above the chair as if he or she is afraid to put weight on it.

Would it be hard to stay in that position for a while if you could not put your whole weight on the chair? **Just as it is hard to "half-way" trust in the chair, we really cannot half-way trust in God. Having faith in God means we completely trust Him to care for us. It goes beyond just believing with our minds; it means being willing to pray to Him and trust Him to do what is right.**

Friendship

40. Same Direction

Run a race, with a little different twist. Pair up kids, and ask them to link arms, but with one person facing one direction and the other one facing the opposite direction. At the instruction to GO, each pair should run toward the wall they are facing, which is the goal line. After a bit of struggling, talk about it. *Why was it so hard to get to your side of the room?* (Because we were linked with someone going the opposite way.)

Run the race again with arms linked going in the same direction.

Was it easier to get to the goal line with both going in the same direction? Yes, of course.

Read 2 Corinthians 6:14. *Why is it important for us to be "linked up" with other believers?* (So we can both go in the right way; so we will not be pulled in the wrong direction, etc.)

Christian friends can help us because we are all going in the right direction.

41. Lean on Me

Ask each family member to find a partner and sit on the floor with their backs to one another (partners of similar height works best, if possible). Instruct each pair to link arms and stand up without unlinking their arms. (They will have to lean on one another to be able to do this.)

How did you help each other so you could both stand up? (We had to lean against one another; we had to push against the other; etc.)

Read Ecclesiastes 4:9-10. *What do these verses tell us about friendship?*

How can we support one another? (Help each other; be a friend; listen; pray for each other; say kind words; etc.)

God gives us others for support. When one needs help, another can help. When one is sad, another can cheer up that person. When one is weak, another one can pray and support. What a gift to have Christian friends!

42. Give and Take

Roll or toss a ball back and forth to help your child see the need to give and take in a friendship. After a few times of back and forth, when your child rolls the ball to you, take it and walk away. When they ask, "Where are you going?" come back and toss the ball some more.

Then talk about it: ***How did you feel when I took the ball and walked away?*** **We cannot play catch with only one person—it takes both of us to throw the ball back and forth. A friendship takes two people. When a friend makes a kind move toward us, we should make a kind move back. If someone gives us a smile, we can smile back. A good friendship requires two people who are willing to give and take.**

43. Talk and Listen

Use a talking stick to teach your kids the valuable skill of waiting for their turn to talk. (You can use a wooden spoon or whatever easily fits in a child's hand that can be passed back and forth; it can be decorated with paper or colored tape, if you like.)

While still at the table after a meal, introduce the talking stick. The one rule: whoever has the talking stick has permission to talk; all others must listen. Pass the stick to someone and allow them to share something about their day or talk about whatever they like. Do not allow anyone to interrupt or say anything while the person is still talking. (Practicing at home is good!) Then pass the talking stick to another child who can talk.

A good friend listens. We all like to share about ourselves, but never listening to our friend is selfish. We must also take time to listen and not interrupt when he/she is sharing.

Read Luke 6:31. ***How does the Bible say we should treat others?*** **We should treat others as we want to be treated. If we want others to listen to us, we must listen to them.**

*Here are a few tips to help your child build good friendships:

- Practice a simple greeting/introduction for your child to use on the playground, etc.
- Brainstorm some simple games or jokes your child can share with other kids.
- Attend church regularly and invite some of your child's classmates to your house.
- Enroll your child in a new class or sport where he or she can meet other kids.
- Stay involved and encourage relationships with kids who share your values.

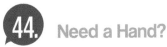

44. Need a Hand?

Gather a box and gift wrapping supplies (newspaper works well for gift wrap). Ask one of the kids to wrap a gift . . . using only one hand (the other must stay behind the back).

After he or she struggles for a little while, ask for a volunteer to help. (They should use one hand also—making a total of two hands wrapping the gift.)

Why was it easier to wrap the gift with someone helping? (He could hold the box; he could tear off the tape; etc.)

We all need others to help us, especially when things are hard.

How can others help us when we are having a hard time? (They can listen; they can pray for us; they can say encouraging words; they can be with us; etc.)

Paul and Timothy worked together to do God's work. Paul spent time with Timothy; he wrote encouraging words to Timothy; he prayed for Timothy. Having good friends can help us do God's work!

45. Stand Together

Try an experiment to see if sticking together makes things better. Ask three family members to stand shoulder to shoulder across the room. Choose one person to stand facing the others. Give him or her three chances to throw a ball past their line. The ball has to be thrown below the shoulder level. (The ones forming the line should do their best to stand tightly together so the ball will not get through.)

Then ask the three to spread across the room (away from each other). Now give the "thrower" three chances to get the ball past the line. Give others a turn to be the "thrower" if you like.

When was it easier to get the ball past the line of family members—when they were close together or when they were far apart? (far apart)

Read Psalm 133:1. ***What does the verse tell us is good?*** (Brothers being united is good.)

Just as it was easier to keep the ball from getting through when everyone stood together, it will be easier to keep out what is wrong and do what is right when we stay close together.

 ## 46. Do Your Part

Put things that kids might argue over (remote control, video game, one cookie, a favorite toy, etc.) in a bag. Pair up family members and let them choose an item from the bag. Give them a few minutes to come up with a short skit about a disagreement over their chosen item. Take turns acting out the skits for each other.

Why do we have disagreements? (We have different ideas and opinions; we want our own way; we think something is not fair; etc.)

Disagreements are going to happen. If there is only one of something, there will be a disagreement!

Here are three steps to solving disagreements.

1. Consider others. (Philippians 2:3-4)

Pride keeps me (and each of us) seeing how I like things, how I do things, or how I want things, instead of how others think or even what God wants. When we consider others' opinions and suggestions, we can work on a solution. The Bible tells us to be humble and consider what others want.

2. Stay calm. (James 1:19-20)

What happens when we get angry? (We say or do wrong things; we may attack the person instead of trying to find a solution; we are not able to listen to others.)

3. Talk it out. (Do not forget to listen.) (Matthew 5:23-24)

When the Christian believers did not agree, they talked about the problem. And remember, there was not just talking, but there was also listening.

Disagreements will happen, but we can work together to find a good solution.

Steps to Forgiveness

Help kids (especially siblings) learn to see the good in one another and forgive. When kids have a spat with one another, ask them to stand on opposite sides of the room, facing each other. Set the timer for two minutes and ask one to share his side of the story while the other listens without interrupting. Set the timer again and allow the other one to share his side, without interrupting. Then ask, *"How can we solve this?"* Reach an agreement and decide to forgive.

Then ask each one to take a step toward the other and say one good thing about the other (something good about the other person or something he enjoys doing with the other) until they are face to face and can shake hands or embrace.

Brotherly love is about forgiving and letting the hurt go (1 Peter 4:8).

 ## Forgive One Another

Memorize a great verse for families: Ephesians 4:32. This verse loosely fits the song "Frère Jacques" ("Are You Sleeping?") repeating phrases as you would in the folk song. (ESV works best, but you can make other translations fit.) Sing the song together to review the verse. Once they have memorized it well enough, try singing it in a round. Divide into two groups, and the second group can begin singing at "tenderhearted."

What is the opposite of tenderhearted? (Hardhearted; not wanting to forgive, but wanting to get revenge.)

Why should we forgive others? (God has forgiven us.)

God's forgiveness to us is the reason we can forgive others. Others have not hurt us more than our sin hurt Jesus. Our sin against God is bigger than any sin that others have done to us. God forgives us; we can forgive others.

Humility

49. All Puffed Up

Sometimes a good way to understand a word is to think about its opposite. The opposite of humility is pride.

What is pride? (Thinking too highly of one's self; thinking you are better than others; etc.)

Invite the kids to think of and say statements that a proud person might say. With each statement, blow a big puff into a balloon (holding it closed until all statements have been added).

- *I am better than anyone on my team.*
- *I bet they wish they were as good as me.*
- *I do not need anybody's help.*
- *She is lucky to have me as her friend.*
- *Why should I have to wait in line?*
- *I do not care what my parents say.*
- *I will do what I want.*
- *She is not as smart as me.*
- *I should get to go first.*

This is a big bag of air. An over-inflated opinion of ourselves pushes others away from us. (Let the air escape.) **Even God resists the proud** (James 4:6). **We need humility. Humility is recognizing that we need God and others.**

50. Do What I Do

Play a game of imitation. Pair up family members and ask them to face one another. Choose one to lead. This person will do simple actions (scratch nose, put hair behind ear, blink eyes, raise arm, etc.) and the other person must imitate that person as quickly and closely as possible. Reverse roles.

Was it easy to follow your partner's example? Why or why not?

We need good examples to follow. Jesus is our example of humility (read Philippians 2:5-8).

How did Jesus model humility for us? (He left Heaven and came to earth; He was considerate of others; He was gentle with young kids; He forgave others; He did not insist on His own way; etc.)

How can we show humility to others? (We can think of others; we can admit when we are wrong; we can talk to others in a kind and gentle manner; etc.)

By following Jesus' example, we can model humility for others.

51. You Go First

Declare this a "You Go First" week. One way to kill pride is to think of others more than we think of ourselves. Challenge family members to look for ways to let others go first.

For example:

- If you are watching TV, let someone else pick the show.
- If you are riding in the car, let someone else choose the "best" seat.
- If you are picking a snack, let someone else choose what they want first.

How did you feel when someone let you go first? (Cared for, happy, etc.)

How did you feel when you let someone go first? (Glad that I was doing the right thing; happy that I could make someone else happy; etc.)

Humility draws other people toward us.

Obedience

52. Easy or Hard?

Is it easy or hard to obey? Is it easy or hard to obey God's rules?

Read the following situations and ask kids to let you know if they think it is easy or hard to obey. Thumbs up is easy; thumbs down shows that it is hard. Or if you want to get them moving, designate sides of the room to go to for each choice.

- Your mom tells you that you can stay up an hour later.
- Your dad tells you to take out the trash.
- Your teacher tells you to go to lunch.
- The Bible tells you to be kind to others.
- Your mom insists you go shopping with her.
- Your dad tells you to take a break from cleaning the garage.
- Your teacher tells you to write a book report.
- Your mom tells you to do the dishes.
- The Bible tells you to forgive others.

Read Ephesians 6:1-3 and Romans 13:1.

What does God want us to do? Sometimes it will be easy and sometimes it will be hard to obey. God wants you to obey—to do what He has asked no matter what.

53. Which Way Do I Go?

Pair up family members and designate one as the listener and the other as the guide. Blindfold the listener and tell the guide that he must direct his partner safely to a designated spot, using words but not touching him. (Take five steps and turn right. Walk straight ahead. Carefully, walk down three steps. Stop, etc.) When the listener has arrived safely at the designated spot, switch roles.

Talk about it:

Did you like being the listener or the guide?

How did your guide's instructions help you? (They helped you know which way to go; they kept you safe; etc.)

What might have happened if you ignored the instructions of the person guiding you? (I could have been hurt; I might have fallen; etc.)

What happened to the people of Israel when they ignored God's instructions? (They suffered terrible consequences. They were conquered by another country; they had to leave their homes; many of them were killed.)

Read Deuteronomy 28:1-2, 15.

What did God promise His people? (If they followed Him, He would bless them; if they would not listen, they would suffer the consequences.)

God told them if they would obey His commands (rules) He would bless them, but they would not listen. Instead they went their own way and had to suffer. Following God's way is always best.

54. Rules Protect

As you are driving, ask:

What might happen if I drove on the wrong side of the road or if I ran a red light or stop sign? (We could get in an accident and someone could get hurt.)

Why should we follow God's rules? (Because they protect us and lead us in the right way.)

God's rules (commandments) actually protect us from getting hurt and can make our lives go much better.

Pick some of the Ten Commandments (Exodus 20) and talk about how they protect us and make our lives better. For example: the eighth commandment, **Do not steal.**

How can keeping this rule protect us? (It protects us from getting in trouble; it can protect us from going to jail; it protects us from a guilty conscience; etc.)

How can obeying God's rule, "Do not lie," protect you? (It keeps you from feeling guilty if you lie; it will protect your reputation so others will not think of you as a liar; it will help others trust what you say; etc.) Talk about other commandments that protect us.

How can keeping God's rules make our lives better? (We will get along with others; we will have a good reputation; others will trust us; etc.)

Joshua 1:8 says that if we meditate on and obey God's rules, we will be happier.

55. Obeying Is Good

Items needed: ingredients to make homemade ice cream in a bag
1 tablespoon sugar
1/2 cup milk or half & half
1/4 teaspoon vanilla
6 tablespoons rock salt (coarse salt works best, but table salt will also work)
1 pint-size sturdy plastic food storage bag
1 gallon-size plastic food storage bag
ice cubes
spoons

INSTRUCTIONS:

1. Fill the large bag half full of ice, and add the rock salt. Seal the bag.
2. Put milk, vanilla, and sugar into the small bag, and **tightly** seal it.
3. Place the small bag inside the large one, and seal it again **carefully**.
4. Shake until the mixture is ice cream, which takes about 5 minutes.
5. Wipe off the top of the small bag, then open it carefully. Enjoy!

Make homemade ice cream in a bag using the instructions. The recipe makes enough for one person. Adjust for the number of people in your family. Pass out spoons and eat the ice cream right from the bag. While eating, talk about it:

Why did we need instructions? (To help us know what to do, how to make it, etc.)

What might have happened if we did not follow the instructions and poured the salt right into the ice cream mixture? (It would have ruined it; it would have tasted bad; etc.)

Why do you think God gives us instructions? (We do not always know what to do, how to live, etc.)

Where can we find God's instructions? (In the Bible)

Why is it hard to follow instructions? (We want our own way; we do not listen; etc.)

We do not always know the right way to live, but God's instructions will help us. What are some instructions we can obey? Read 1 Thessalonians 5:12-22.

56. Learn From Others

Tell your kids about a time when you disobeyed your parents (and possibly share the consequences). Tell them it is not always easy to obey because we are born with a desire to sin. That is why Jesus came to die for our sins and to live inside us to help us.

Teach them 1 John 1:9. (If we confess our sins, He is faithful and just to forgive us our sins, and to cleanse us from all unrighteousness.)

Teach them to say a simple prayer. **Dear God, I am sorry for _____ (name the sin). Please help me to do what is right. Amen.**

57. Obey/Reward

Write each of the following Bible addresses on a piece of paper: Ephesians 6:1; Ephesians 4:32; Philippians 4:4; 1 Thessalonians 5:18; Ephesians 4:29.

Write each of the following rewards on a piece of paper: Stay up 30 minutes later; play a game together; skip chore; pick 3 books to read; pick a dessert that you like; etc.

Read one verse each morning at breakfast and challenge the kids to obey the command in the verse that day. Try to catch them obeying the verse and talk about how they did every night at dinner. If they have done well, allow them to pick a reward card.

58. Obey the Instructions

Hide a reward (treat of food, bag of cookies, small gift, whatever you like) at a specific destination without the kids knowing it. Announce that there is a reward hidden for them but they must follow your instructions to get it. (All the kids can do this together or you can do it one at a time if you have a smaller family.) Verbally give clues a little at a time (go ten steps and turn left; look until you find a yellow flower; go where there is something we use to cut the grass; etc.) or write them on slips of paper and give them at the appropriate time.

After the reward has been found and enjoyed, talk about it:

What might have happened if you had NOT followed the instructions? (We would not have found the reward; we would have wandered around; etc.)

Why are instructions important? (They help us find the way; they help us know how things work; they guide us, etc.)

Where are God's instructions? (Bible)

Why is it good for us to obey God's instructions? (So we can know the wise way to live; so we can know how to get along with others; so we can know how to love God; etc.)

Read Psalm 19:9-11.

What do these verses tell us about God's law/words? (They are true, fair, better than gold or honey, and there is a reward for keeping them.)

God's instructions are found in the Bible, and there is a great reward when we follow them!

59. This Is the Way We . . .

Build good habits to help your kids become more disciplined. Habits help everyone know what to do and follow through with less effort. (I still cannot go to bed without brushing my teeth, or at least without hearing my mom's voice making me get out of bed to do it!)

What are some good habits?

Brush your teeth. Pray before a meal. Say a prayer before bedtime. Sing in the car. Read the Bible at the breakfast table. Hang up your coat. Make your bed. Do your homework right after school.

What is important to you? Those are the habits to teach. Pick one a week and start!

60. Remember the Commands

Make and play a memory game to find commands to be obeyed. Cut index cards in half or cut squares from construction paper to make 20 squares or just use Post-It® notes. Give each child two squares and instruct them to write the command on both cards. Continue until all the cards are filled. Turn the cards face down, mix them up, and put them in rows. Choose one person to go first and turn over two cards to see if they match. If not, turn them back over and the next person has a turn. The one with the most matches at the end is the winner.

Bible commands to be obeyed:
Love God. (Deuteronomy 6:5)
Be thankful. (Colossians 3:15)
Read the Bible. (1 Timothy 4:13)
Rejoice in the Lord. (Psalm 32:11)
Pray. (Psalm 32:6)
Obey your parents. (Ephesians 6:1)
Tell the gospel (good news). (Matthew 28:19)
Love your neighbor. (Matthew 22:39)
Forgive one another. (Colossians 3:13)
Speak the truth. (Proverbs 12:19)

61. Excuses, Excuses

Make up a story about Ethan, the Expert Excuse-maker. Start the story by saying something Ethan needs to do (get out of bed, eat his breakfast, put his shoes on, take the dog outside, etc.) and then give a real or outlandish excuse why he cannot do it.

For example:

First person: Whenever Ethan was told to do something, he ALWAYS made an excuse. When his mom said, "Get out of bed, it is time for school," Ethan said, "I can't. There's a dragon sitting on top of my chest."

The next person will continue the story and add another thing Ethan needs to do and give an excuse why he cannot do it.

Go around adding situations and excuses.

Ask:

Why do we give excuses? (We do not want to do it; we do not think we can do it; we are afraid; etc.)

God met Moses at a burning bush and laid out a plan for Moses. God wanted Moses to go to Pharaoh and tell him to free the Israelites from slavery.

Read Exodus 3:10-14; 4:1, 10-14. *What are some of the excuses Moses gave?*

(I cannot do this; I doubt anyone will listen to me; I am not good at talking to others; please send someone else to do it.)

Even though Moses made excuses, he finally obeyed and said yes to God's plan, and the Israelites were freed from slavery.

62. Keep Trying

Play a Minute-to-Win-It game to talk about determination and not quitting. Give each player 25 M&Ms (or Skittles), a straw, and two paper plates. Players must place a straw in their mouth and use suction to transfer a pile of 25 M&Ms from one plate to another in under one minute. (Use only one hand to hold the straw.) If they cannot get all the M&Ms transferred in one minute, give them more chances to keep trying. (You may need to adjust the number for younger kids.) When finished, talk about it and eat the candy!

Ask:

How did you feel as you were trying to transfer the candy in one minute?

How did you feel when you were finally able to do it?

You were determined. *What does it mean to be determined?* **To be determined means that you do not give up, no matter what. You keep trying. Even when it is hard, keep going and do not give up!**

Optional: Depending on the ages of your kids, pick an appropriate task (stack so many blocks or Starburst pieces, move so many cotton balls from one plate to another, etc.).

63. Who Can Last?

Hold an endurance contest; see who can go the longest without biting their Tootsie Pop. As you are licking, talk about how hard it is to wait.

What was the hardest part of the contest? Why?

Why is it so hard to keep waiting? What are some things we can do while we wait?

We want what we want when we want it! But sometimes we need to put aside what we want (or what we feel like doing) and do what is right!

64. Don't Quit

Announce that you want to play a game. Get out the game board and about halfway through the game, say, "I quit" and walk away. (The kids will be yelling, "That's not fair! You can't do that!")

Come back to the table and ask:

How did you feel when I quit the game?

Why is it important to stick with something to the end?

Jesus said that people who want to be His disciples must stick with it. They must count the cost and be sure that they are willing to follow Him. There are some who want to quit when things are hard, but a true follower of Jesus stays with Him no matter what (Luke 14:27).

Do not forget to come back to the table and FINISH the game—even if you do not win.

Optional:

Quit any job in the middle—quit making dinner, cut half the yard and put the mower away, etc. When the kids notice, ask them why it is important to stay with something until it is finished.

65. Keep at It

Have a contest to see which "pair" can bat a balloon back and forth the longest without it touching the floor. (Let the rest watch and count as the balloon hits each person's hand.) Take turns letting another pair give it a try.

Ask:

What was the hardest part of doing this? (Concentrating, getting tired, not knowing where the balloon was going, etc.)

Loving and serving God requires staying power.

Let each person tell one goal (related to their spiritual life) that they would like to do (read the Bible every day, obey the first time asked, help someone each week, etc.). Write them down and bring them out the first day of each week to see if everyone is still staying with it.

66. With All Your Heart

Make two lists: a chore/job list and a reward list. Write a different chore on a slip of paper (enough for each member of the family to have at least one) and put them in a jar or bag. Write a different reward (stay up 30 minutes later at bedtime, choose a game to play, pick the dinner menu, choose a snack at the store, pick a small treat, etc.) on each slip of paper and put them in a second jar or bag.

Gather the family and show them the two jars. Explain that each person will pick a chore and then will be able to choose a reward when it is completed.

Read Colossians 3:23-24.

How should we do our tasks? (Heartily, with a good attitude, do it as if we are doing it for God)

Will there be a reward for our faithfulness to God? (Yes, not always right away, but certainly when we go to Heaven)

 67. Incomplete

Ask the kids to put together a puzzle, but hold back several pieces (without their knowing it). When they get to the end and realize that several pieces are missing, give them the other pieces.

Why was it hard to put the puzzle together? (Some of the pieces were missing.)

Some parts of life are like a puzzle. We see things happening that just do not make sense. Sometimes people do WRONG things and it seems they get away with it. Sometimes people do the RIGHT thing and they have trouble.

Read Romans 8:28. (If you have older kids, also read Romans 8:23-27.)

What does God promise? (All things will work together for good to those who love Him.) Notice this does not say that all things are good, but that God will cause good to come from them.

Even though we do not understand why something is happening, we can still trust God. Someday we will see God, and there will be no more pain or sadness in Heaven. Then the picture will be complete. Remembering this can give us hope when we do not understand why something is happening.

68. Test It

Fill a shoebox with books (to the top) and tape it shut. (Make sure that the kids do not see you doing this.) Set the box on the floor and ask, *"What will happen if you stand on the box?"* Tell them the box will not cave in and ask them to trust you, to believe that you are telling the truth. Invite one of the kids to test it and stand on it.

Why didn't the box cave in? Show them the books inside holding it up. Say something like this:

Even though you did not know there were books in it, you trusted me even though it seemed impossible that it would not cave in. Faith means believing what God says is true. God can be trusted. The Bible is God's Word and it is reliable. God wants us to believe Him even when we do not understand what is happening. He knows things that we do not and has a plan that is best.

69. Good/Bad

Gather ingredients to make cookies. Let the kids taste the individual ingredients (salt, baking soda, butter, flour, etc.) before mixing them together. Ask how each one tastes.

Mix and bake the cookies. Eat the cookies with some cold milk. Ask how they liked them.

Ask:

What are some things in life that are not good? (Sickness, sadness, hurt feelings, loneliness, etc.)

There was a man in the Bible named Job who had a lot of trouble (Job 1 and 2). **His children died, his animals died, and he lost his good health. Even his friends accused him of doing wrong things.** *Was everything in Job's life good?* **No, he had some very bad things happen to him and his family.**

What happened at the end of Job's life? Read Job 42:12-13. **God blessed Job and gave him more animals, children, and good things than he had before.**

Is everything in life good? (No.) **Just as the ingredients we tasted by themselves were not so good, we were able to make something good from them. God is so wise and powerful that He can take even the bad things that happen and make something good from them.**

70. The Rock

Ask kids to go outside and find a rock they like. (This will be a reminder to them that God's promises are strong and sure, so it needs to be more than a pebble. One about the size of a hand is good.)

Read Matthew 7:24-27. **Jesus said that whoever heard His words and did them would be like a man who built his house on a strong rock. When the storms came, the house did not fall apart. Another man built his house on sand, and the house fell apart when the storms came.**

If we live by God's words, we will have strength to face the storms (trouble) that come. If we live by our own way and feelings, we will not be strong. If we believe and live by God's promises, they can protect us when trouble comes. By putting God's promises in our mind and thinking about them, we can be hopeful when sad and worried feelings come.

How are God's promises like a rock? (They are strong and sure, not always changing; they last a long time; they are strong enough to build on.)

Write a message or a Bible verse on the rock and keep it as a reminder to keep God's promises in our minds. Here are some good promise verses: Hebrews 13:5b; Psalm 27:1; Romans 8:28; Jeremiah 31:3.

71. Heart to Heart

Before prayer at bedtime, ask your child:

Are you going through a difficult situation?

Are you having a hard time doing the right thing?

Do you need God's help?

Share with your kids about a hard time you had (a temptation that God helped you overcome, a trial where you felt distant from God, a time of need when you wondered whether God was going to help you). Share what helped you get through it.

Pray Numbers 6:24-26 for your child *("The Lord bless you and keep you; the Lord make His face shine on you and be gracious to you; the Lord turn His face toward you and give you peace." NIV).* Give him/her a big hug and a short back rub!

Knowing that parents are in their corner, cheering them on and praying for them, can give kids what they need to keep going. Remembering how you have felt in hard times and sharing that can build a close connection.

72. What Is Prayer?

Read Matthew 6:5-6.

Jesus told His followers that prayer is a conversation, not a show for others to watch. He told them to find a quiet place (a closet, possibly) and talk to Him.

Is it hard to pray because we cannot see God? Pull an empty chair across from you. Ask family members to imagine that Jesus is sitting in a chair across from them. *What would you say to Him?*

Jesus is our Friend who wants to hear about our day, who wants to help us, who wants to comfort us, who can answer our requests. We must take the time to talk to Him.

73. Pretzel Prayers

Share a simple object lesson about prayer using a pretzel. Make pretzels together or use purchased ones. (For this object lesson, make or choose the knots/twisted ones.)

Although no one is exactly sure when and where pretzels were first made, there is a story that long ago there was a kind Italian monk who knew how important prayer was. He cut long strips of baked dough and folded them into a special shape, the shape of crossed arms (which is what they did when they prayed). Then he baked and gave them to the children as rewards for saying their prayers.

Ask them to hold out their arms in front and then cross their arms across their chest. Teach them a simple prayer, having them repeat each line after you.

I bow my head (bow head),
And twist my arms tight (cross arms across chest).
I ask God to help me
Say and do what's right.

I say a prayer
To my Father above,
To give Him thanks
For His great love.

Eat the pretzels. Every day we need God's help to do what is right. God wants us to talk to Him and He listens. We can ask Him for what we need.

74. God's Hands

Decorate a shoe box (or box of similar size) to hold prayer requests. Write the words, "God's hands" on the shoebox.

Ask:

What could you do if your toy or something you own breaks? (You could give it to someone who knows how to fix it.)

When we have problems too big for us to handle, we can put our problems in "God's hands." God is wise and knows what is best. We can trust Him to help us.

Allow kids to write down a request on a slip of paper. Fold it and put it in the box. Say a prayer asking God for help and for His will to be done in that situation. Pray for the requests in the box each day, asking God to work out His will.

Read Jeremiah 33:3.

What does God promise to do? (Great and mighty things) **We may not know what God will do (and it may not be exactly what we want), but God will do what is best.**

75. The Lord's Prayer

Grab some paper (copy or construction paper) and markers or crayons to illustrate the Lord's Prayer. Write a phrase from the Lord's Prayer (Matthew 6:9-13) at the top of each paper. Invite the kids to choose a phrase and illustrate it. If they are younger, brainstorm with them to give them ideas on how to draw what the phrase means.

When finished, let each one read the phrase and show their picture. Post the pictures in order in a prominent spot (tape them on a long piece of yarn or twine to make a banner) and say the prayer together once a day for the rest of the week.

76. Record It

Start a prayer journal. Buy a spiral notebook. Draw a vertical line down the middle of the page and on one side write, *Date Asked* and on the other side, *Date Answered*. Every evening after dinner, take a few minutes to pray. Write the requests in the notebook. Then say sentence prayers asking God to answer the requests. Record the date requested and the date answered. (You could do this at bedtime if your family gathers together then.)

Howard Hendricks, a Christian author, said he did this when his children were growing up and this is one of the most valuable things they own. It is his legacy to his children as evidence that God is real and hears and answers prayer.

77. P.R.A.Y.

Use the word "PRAY" as a guide in praying.

P raise God!

Draw a picture to express your thoughts about God or say your own words of praise to Him. (If you need ideas, read Psalm 145.)

R epent!

To repent means that you are sorry for your sin and you want to change. Sit quietly and think. Is there any sin I need to repent of? If you need God to take away any sin, tell Him that you are sorry and ask Him to forgive you (1 John 1:9).

A sk

Ask God for whatever you or your family or friends need. Say or write three requests. Put today's date and wait to see how God will answer (Philippians 4:6).

Y ield

To yield to God means that you say "yes" to what He wants. Tell God that you want His will more than you want your own way (Romans 12:1-2).

78. See and Pray

Make a picture prayer book, especially if you have younger children. Put pictures of family members and friends (print digital photos) in a small photo album or notebook. Look at the pictures at prayer time and choose one or several for prayer. Think of specific requests for each one.

 79. Different Ways

The Bible gives many different positions for prayer. Look up the verses to find a way to pray, and then pray that way. Or you could tack up each verse at a different place, find each one, read the verse, and say a short prayer at each spot.

- Psalm 123:1 (eyes open and looking toward Heaven)
- Psalm 95:6 (kneeling)
- Psalm 63:4 (lifting up your hands)
- Deuteronomy 9:18 (lying on the floor)

Call out to God wherever you are, no matter the position of your body. The praying position is not as important as what you are thinking or saying. God cares more about your heart (1 Samuel 16:7).

80. Simple Prayers

If you have younger children, teach them the habit of saying a prayer before their meal. Here are some I said when I was a child. Simple, regular prayers can build a good habit and discipline in our kids.

God is great!
God is good!
Let us thank Him
For our food.
Amen.
– Traditional

Thank you for the world so sweet;
Thank you for the food we eat.
Thank you for the birds that sing;
Thank you, God, for everything.
– Author Unknown

Here is a simple song for young children to pray before meals to acknowledge God as the Father who meets our needs. An easy way to teach it is to sing each phrase and have them repeat it after you.

(Sing to tune, "Are You Sleeping?")

God, our Father, (God, our Father,)
Once again (once again)
We bow our heads to thank you. (We bow our heads to thank you.)
Amen (Amen).

81. Follow His Example

Pray Bible prayers for others. Write out the names of family and friends on slips of paper. Write out ideas of prayers to pray on slips of paper (keeping the two stacks separate). Put the two stacks in two bowls. Every evening after dinner (or at bedtime), choose one slip from each bowl and pray the prayer for the person drawn.

Some ideas of prayers from the Bible (Jesus' prayer in John 17 and Paul's prayer in Ephesians 1):

- Protect them (John 17:11)
- Give them joy (John 17:13)
- Keep them safe from the evil one (John 17:15)
- Make them holy by God's Word (John 17:16-17)
- Fill them with God's love (John 17:26)
- They will be united and work together (John 17:21)
- They will be wise (Ephesians 1:17)
- They will grow in the knowledge of God (Ephesians 1:17)

Jesus prays for us! We can follow His example and pray for others.

 82. Jesus Is Our Safe Place

Play hide and seek in the backyard to illustrate God's protection from sin. Designate a specific point (a tree or shed or whatever) as the base, a "safe" place. When anyone gets to the safe place, he is safe and cannot be caught. Choose one person to be "it" who will hide his eyes and count to 20. Everyone else should find a hiding place. The object of the game is to get to the safe place. (Let your little ones get to the safe place as often as possible.)

When tired of the game, sit on the grass and talk.

How did it feel to make it to the safe place without getting caught? (Good, relieved, happy, etc.)

How is Jesus our safe place? (When we accept Jesus, we do not have to be punished for our sins. He will bring us to Heaven to live with Him forever.)

All who believe in Jesus will have their sins taken away and will be with Him forever in Heaven (the ultimate safe place).

Read John 3:16. Say a prayer of thanks to Jesus for being a safe place.

83. Grace: A Gift

To help your kids understand the concept of grace, give each child a gift card to spend. Take them to the store (or a restaurant if that is where the card is from) to let them use it. (An optional idea is to buy a small gift for each one.)

Talk about it:

What did you do to earn the gift card? (Nothing; it was a GIFT.)

A gift is not earned. A gift does not cost you anything. *Who paid for your gift card?* (Mom, Dad) **Someone else pays the price of the item when he/she gives you a gift.**

Read Ephesians 2:8-9.

How is this like what Jesus did for us? (He paid the price for our sin so we could have salvation.) **God's gift of salvation is free to us; Jesus paid the price so we could be forgiven. We cannot earn it; it is a gift!**

84   Jesus Offers New Life

Bring out your child's baby book and birth certificate and talk about the day he or she was born into your family. (Kids never seem to tire of hearing about themselves.) Show pictures and talk about how happy you were. If they were adopted, talk about the happy day they became a part of your family.

Ask:

How do you become part of God's family? How are you born again?

Read John 3:1-16 to review Jesus' conversation with Nicodemus.

Simple truths about being "born into God's family":

- God loves you and wants you to be in His family (John 3:16).
- We have all sinned and gone our own way (Romans 3:23).
- Jesus came to earth and died on the cross for our sins (1 John 4:10).
- We have to believe that He died for our sins and came alive again (Romans 10:9).
- Tell God that you want to receive Him into your life; we need to receive His forgiveness for our sins.
- Say thank you to Him. Celebrate!

If they understand the basic truths about salvation, individually ask:

Would you like to receive Jesus into your life? (Doing this on a one-on-one basis is best, not in a group.)

85.   I Am _____

While you are driving in the car, guess the identity of famous people. Announce a category of famous people that your kids would know (historical figures/presidents, TV personalities, cartoon characters, singers, etc.) and invite one person at a time to pick a person (but not tell anyone). The others will ask questions that can only be answered by a yes or no to discover their person's identity. (Am I a man? Am I still living? Could you see me on TV? Am I famous for singing? etc.)

If you have younger kids, you may want to guess animals instead of people. Give them clues if they need help after a few minutes.

Talk about it:

What is an identity? (Who you are, what you are like, etc.)

Read 2 Corinthians 5:17. **When a person accepts and follows Jesus, he is a new creation. He/she has a new identity. No, you do not get a new name or body, but you are different on the inside. God forgives your sin and makes you part of His family. We are to live in ways that honor God and our new family. The old ways of selfishness should be put away and the new ways of loving should be part of who we are.**

86. He Is Always With You

Many children are unsure about their salvation and tend to want to invite Jesus in again and again. Second Peter 1:5-9 says that if you keep growing (adding good things to your life like faith, knowledge, self-control, patience, goodness, kindness, and love), you can be sure you are a Christ follower.

One way I have explained this to children is by having one child go outside the room or house and knock on the door. I go to the door, invite the child in, and sit down and begin to talk. As we are talking, I say to the child, "Come in, Susan." Of course, she will probably say, "I'm already in." Talk a little more and say again, "Come in, Susan."

Explain that you only need to invite Jesus into your life one time. You DO need to say, "I'm sorry," when you sin, but Jesus does not leave you. Sin makes Him sad, but He is still with you. If they keep adding good things, they will grow in assurance.

87. Two Birthdays!

Celebrate SECOND birthdays—the day your kids were born into God's family. Put it on the calendar and treat it as a very special day. (If you do not know the specific day, pick a date as close as you can remember.)

- Make a birthday cake with candles indicating how many years they have been in God's family.
- Enjoy a special meal.
- Talk about what it means to have faith in Jesus and be part of His family.
- Say a special prayer of blessing.
- Mention ways that you see them growing in faith and being more like Jesus.
- Give a gift that will help them to grow spiritually (CD, devotional magazine or book, Bible, etc.).
- CELEBRATE! Make it a fun day! (It may create a chance to share the gospel with others.)

88. I Can't Wait

Make a bowl of popcorn the old-fashioned way. (If you do not have kernels to pop, microwave popcorn will also work as even waiting a couple of minutes is a long time for a kid!) Stand by the microwave or stove waiting for it to pop. When it is done, let it cool a little and eat it together.

If you are really brave, pop the kernels on the stove but leave the lid off. Hold the corners of a clean bed sheet nearby to catch the kernels as they fly through the air. (Do not try to catch the kernels in your mouth since they are very hot.)

(This would work with making any food when there is a waiting time—making popsicles, making a pot of soup, or baking a cake or loaf of bread.)

Ask:

Why is it so hard to wait? (I want to eat it now; I am hungry; it takes too long; etc.)

Read Galatians 5:22-23. ***Which of these might you need if you have a hard time waiting?*** (Depending on the translation: patience, forbearance, longsuffering.) **Patience is being able to wait without getting angry or upset. It is very hard to be patient.**

How do you get patience? **The Bible says trials—hard times—produce patience. No one really likes hard times, but James 1:2-3 says we should be glad to have trials because they can produce patience in us.**

When do you need patience? (When you have to wait in line; when you have to keep quiet and just listen in class; when you have to do a hard job, etc.) **Waiting gives us a chance to learn and practice patience.**

89. Oh No! A Wrong Reaction

Do a simple experiment to show how our anger can grow and hurt others.

Gather needed items: cup or glass, liquid dishwashing detergent, two tablespoons of baking soda, vinegar, red food coloring (optional), baking pan (or do this in the sink).

- Fill the cup/glass almost full with warm water.
- Add several drops of the red food coloring and a few drops of the liquid detergent.
- Add 2 tablespoons of baking soda.
- Slowly pour vinegar into the cup and jump back quickly!

This reminds me of how anger works in us!

How does this chemical reaction remind you of anger? (It spilled over the container like mean words spill out of the mouth; it is out of control; etc.)

What are some things that can happen when you get angry? (Say mean words, hit, push, fight, etc.)

What can you do when you feel anger building in you? (Pray, keep your mouth shut, be careful of what you say, walk away)

Read James 3:2-8.

It is difficult to tame the tongue. When you are angry, it is easy to lose self-control and say wrong things that can hurt others. You can let your anger build until you say or do things you will be sorry for later. It is a sin to hurt others with your words or actions when you get angry. It is better to stop and pray, watch what you say, and maybe walk away.

(If your kids want to know what happened . . . it is a chemical reaction. When baking soda and vinegar mix, it produces a chemical reaction that produces carbon dioxide—the same gas that bubbles in a real volcano. The gas bubbles build and cause the liquid to overflow.)

 ## 90. Money Talks

Siblings/families can sometimes get lax in the words said to one another. Call a family meeting and talk about which words are permitted and which are not.

"I don't like what you are doing" might be permitted;
"I hate you" is not.

Make sure everyone contributes and decides on what is acceptable and what is not.

Give each person a roll of quarters (or dimes or nickels). Announce that every time they say unkind words, they must forfeit a coin. At the end of the week, the money they have left is theirs to keep or spend.

A good verse to say each morning:

Let the words of my mouth and the meditation of my heart be acceptable in your sight, O Lord, my rock and my redeemer. (*Psalm 19:14 ESV)

 ## 91. Can't Do It

Gather a tube of toothpaste and a paper plate. To illustrate that some things cannot be UN-done when we lose control, invite one of the kids to squirt the toothpaste onto the plate. THEN, instruct him to put it all back in the tube.

When he cannot, ask:

Are there times when we say or do things that we cannot UN-do?

When you get angry and say mean words, can you take back those mean words? (NO, even though you may apologize, the words have been said and probably will be remembered.)

What can you do BEFORE you lose control and say the wrong thing? (Pray, count to 10 or more, keep your mouth shut, walk away)

Read James 1:19-21.

What does the Bible tell us to do? (Be quick to listen, slow to speak, and slow to anger.) **There are some words and actions we cannot UN-do. Think and ask God for help before you say or do wrong things.**

Serving

92. Family Resemblance

Grab the art supplies and ask family members to draw a picture of the person that they think they look most like. (Mom and Dad can also draw pictures.) After each one has shown their picture, switch and talk about other characteristics—not physical ones.

What are some of your good characteristics that you share with other family members? (Sarah is like Aunt Jane, who is very loving. Mark is very honest like Dad.)

Read Acts 10:38.

What did Jesus do while He was on the earth? (He went around doing good.)

As part of His family, we can be like Jesus by doing good things for others.

93. Serving

Jesus told His followers that the way to serve Him is to serve others (Matthew 25:34-45). **Doing good works is not the way to be right with God, but we should do good works when we become a Christ follower** (Ephesians 2:8-10).

Brainstorm ways to serve others this week and then pick an idea or two to do.

Invite another family to join you; it will double the fun and be half the work!

Some ideas to get you started:

- Fill plastic bags with items homeless people might need. Put the bags in your car and give them out when opportunity comes.
- Go to a food pantry and help sort the food.
- Put on rubber gloves and pick up trash at a neighborhood park.
- Make cards and give them out at a nursing home.
- Donate good, used toys to the Salvation Army or a shelter.
- Do yard work for the elderly or handicapped.
- Make appreciation cards and take them to the fire or police station.
- Plant flowers at the church or for an elderly person.
- Make and serve a meal to someone sick or in need of encouragement.

94. Look Out!

Grab a stack of old paper (copy paper, newspaper, or magazines) and stage a battle. Divide family members into two teams and mark a line down the middle of the room (with masking tape or with a row of chairs). Tell them when you say go, they will have one minute to make and throw as many paper balls as they can at the other team. Yell, "Stop!" and then have each team count the paper balls on their side. The team with the fewest number on their side wins.

How did you feel with all those paper balls coming at you?

How is life like a battle? (Even when you want to do the right thing, temptations keep coming at you to do wrong; you feel like wrong things are being constantly thrown at you; etc.)

We are in a spiritual battle! There is a battle going on inside us and we are constantly tempted to do wrong things.

Re-enact the "battle" but give each person a chance to find a shield (piece of cardboard, cookie sheet, trash can or storage bin lid, etc.)

How did having a shield protect you? (I used it to deflect the paper balls; the balls did not hit me; etc.)

God's Word, the Bible, is a shield to protect us. When we read and memorize the Bible, it can help us fight against sin and help us do what is right.

95. Get Ready

As your kids get ready for school, pantomime putting on the armor of God (from Ephesians 6:11-18).

The Bible tells us to put on special "clothing" (armor) to protect us from the wrong things that come against us. This special clothing is not like the clothing we can see and hold, but it reminds us of something we need as we start the day.

Say the following or similar statements for each piece.

- I will strap on the belt of truth—I will tell the truth in every situation.
- I will do what is right (breastplate) even though it is hard.
- My feet will take me to share the good news about Jesus with others.
- I will put up my shield and believe God.
- I will put on the helmet to remember that I have been saved from sin.
- I will use my sword and speak God's Word when I am tempted.

96. A Trap

Show a mouse trap to introduce the idea that sin is a trap.

What do we use to catch the mouse? (Cheese, peanut butter, or whatever you choose)

When the mouse sees the "bait" and goes after it, what happens? (He gets caught!)

How is sin like a trap? (It entices us with something we want; it traps us and it is hard to quit that sin; it is a trick that is not good for us, etc.)

We are all tempted (it is not a sin to be tempted), but when we give in to temptation and do what is wrong, we sin.

After dinner, talk about what we could do when tempted in order to keep from giving in to sin.

You want a pack of gum at the store but do not have any money.
You are tempted to look at a friend's test paper when you do not know the answer.
You feel angry at your mom when she would not let you go to a friend's house.
Your little brother is annoying; you want to scream at him to leave you alone.
You are supposed to clean your room; instead you want to play a game.

Read 1 Corinthians 10:13. **All of us are tempted, but God will make a way for us to escape and not give in. We can ask for God's help every time we are tempted.**

97. Peer Pressure

Is it hard for you to do what is right when others around you are not? **It is hard for all of us!**

Grab markers and paper and make three signs (to illustrate three ways) to deal with peer pressure.

KEEP OUT! Keep out of a situation that you know could lead to trouble. Avoid those people or situations!

WALK OUT! When one person or a group is trying to influence you to do something that is wrong, be prepared to walk out. It may not be easy to walk out or walk away, but remember you don't answer to others for your actions; you answer to God.

SPEAK OUT! Stick up for what you like or believe! Say something!

Brainstorm some things to say. Some suggestions:
- *Everyone is different and that is a good thing.*
- *How would you feel if someone said that to you?*
- *I am not comfortable with that. I need to go.*
- *Let's change the subject; I do not want to talk about that.*
- *I am your friend and I do not want to see you get into trouble.*
- Think of a better idea and suggest that.

Brainstorm what you might say or do in the following situations:

- Others are saying bad things about their parents.
- Your teacher says we all evolved.
- Someone says, "Let's take that candy bar; no one is looking."
- Your friends want to watch a TV show that your parents forbid you to watch.
- Your friends are making fun of someone.
- Others ask, "Why do you believe in a God you cannot see?"

98. Strong Inside

Do a simple science experiment to show how the Holy Spirit living inside can help us to be stronger and win over temptation.

Items needed: Two balloons, not inflated (two paper/plastic cups will also work)
Candle or matches
Water

- Inflate one of the balloons and tie it.
- Put about ¼ cup of water in the other balloon; inflate and tie it.
- Light the candle (or light a match) and hold it under the balloon WITHOUT the water (very closely—it is okay if the flame even touches the balloon).
- Hold the balloon WITH water over the candle or match.

Why does one balloon pop and one does not? Why does the balloon with no water break in the flame? The flame heats whatever is placed in it, so it heats both balloons. The rubber of the balloon without water became so hot that it was too weak to resist the pressure of the air inside the balloon, so it popped.

Why doesn't the balloon with water in it pop when heated by the flame? The water absorbs most of the heat from the flame, so the rubber of the balloon does not become very hot. Since the rubber does not become hot, it does not weaken, and the balloon does not pop.

Ask:

How did filling the balloon with something (water) make it stronger?

How can you be stronger if you are filled with the Holy Spirit?

After Jesus died and came alive again, He told His disciples that He would send someone to help them, to comfort them, and to guide them. That someone is the Holy Spirit. The Bible teaches that when a person becomes a Christian, God's Holy Spirit comes to live inside.

You were born with a desire to sin, but the Holy Spirit can help you fight against sin. The Holy Spirit is the author of the Bible, and He can use God's Word to help you know the right way to live. Every time you say "no" to your own selfish way and "yes" to the Holy Spirit, you become stronger. He will help you to be more loving, peaceful, joyful, gentle, humble, and self-controlled (Galatians 5:22-23). **Ask for His help every day. God can change you from the inside out.**

99. How High?

After your child has given in to temptation and you have a chance to talk alone, ask **"How do you feel when you sin? What does God think about your sin?"**

Read Psalm 103:8-14.

Sometimes we are ashamed to tell God when we do wrong because we think He will be mad at us. God understands us and loves us even when we do wrong. A correct view of God leads to a correct view of ourselves and our sin.

100. Where to Go

Where do we find help in the Bible when we are tempted to . . . ? Post these and look up the verses (and memorize them) to use when temptation comes.

- Worry: Philippians 4:6-7
- Dishonor/disobey parents: Ephesians 6:1
- Steal: Ephesians 4:28
- Lie: Ephesians 4:25
- Covet: Hebrews 13:5
- Hate: Matthew 5:44-45
- Be proud: Philippians 2:3
- Be selfish: Philippians 2:4
- Get angry: Ephesians 4:26-27
- Get revenge: Ephesians 4:32
- Complain: Philippians 2:14

Bonus Section

We have more great ideas to share!

 101. Something to Live Up To

The novel *Little Men,* by Louisa May Alcott, tells about Jo Bhaer and the students at Plumfield Estate School. Every Sunday (I think), Jo would spend time with each one and talk about their behavior the previous week. She would show the student what she had written in a notebook—the good things he/she had done that week.

Always be on the lookout for good things your children do and bless them with your words. Print their name vertically on a piece of paper. Write one good characteristic (that you see in your child) for each letter in their name. To make it easier, the word does not have to start with the letter, just so the letter is used somewhere in the word. For example:

       Available to God
     e**N**thusiastic
    ho**N**est

Hang it on their door or in a prominent place as a reminder of the good characteristics you see in them.

Thankfulness

102. God Gives Good Gifts

After dinner, invite family members to leave the table, choose one thing they are glad God has given them, and hide it (while the others are not looking). Take turns looking for each person's item as they give you clues telling if you are "hot" or "cold."

Take turns allowing each family member to say thank you to God for the item he or she chose and hid.

God is good and gives us what we need! We respond to Him by being thankful.

103. Three Good Things

Complaining can become a habit, so help kids learn to be thankful by making a new rule:

For every complaint, they must say three good things.

Why do we always have mashed potatoes? I do not like lumpy potatoes.

Three good things. . .

- I am glad we have peas. They are my favorite.
- I am happy we have plenty of food to eat.
- I am glad Mom makes dinner for us.

Read what the Bible writer, Paul, learned about contentment in Philippians 4:11-13. **Whether he had plenty or not enough, he learned to be happy (content) in every situation. We can always find something for which to be thankful.**

104. Categories

As you are riding in the car, play "thankful categories." Pick a letter of the alphabet. Take turns naming one thing you are thankful for starting with that letter. Keep going until no one can think of anything else (G: God, grapes, girls, giraffes, etc.). Let another person pick a letter and start again naming things that you are thankful for that begin with that letter. End the game by arriving at your destination or saying, "Wow, God made a lot of things to be thankful for. Thank You, God."

105. A-Z

Grab some markers and a long piece of paper (or poster board or pieces of copy paper taped together)—long enough to write the letters of the alphabet vertically.

Across the top of the paper write, "I am thankful for. . ." Write the letters of the alphabet vertically under the title. Tape the paper to the fridge. Invite the kids to write something they are thankful for on the paper anytime they think of it. (You can write more than one thing beside each letter if you like.)

When you have written one thing for each letter, read the list aloud as a prayer of thanks to our great, giving God.

106. Don't Forget

Stick Post-It® notes on your blessings.

We use Post-It® notes to help us remember things. Did you know the idea for the Post-It® note was thought of in church? In 1974, Arthur Fry was singing in the choir. He could not remember all the numbers for the songs they were going to sing, so he used little pieces of paper to mark the pages, but the pieces of paper kept falling out.

Mr. Fry was a scientist at 3M Company. He remembered that four years earlier another scientist, Spencer Silver, had made a weak adhesive—one that was super weak instead of super strong. It stuck to objects but could easily be lifted off. Mr. Fry used some of it to coat his markers and … success! The adhesive held the markers in place but was easily lifted without damaging the page. Today the Post-It® is one of the most popular school and office supplies.

Give each family member five or so Post-It® notes and ask them to stick them to something they consider a blessing.

Blessings are things that bring happiness/joy to us. God gives us many things to enjoy. Every good gift comes from God (James 1:17).

107. A Good Way to End the Day

Start a new habit. Every night, before bed, ask, **"What three things are you thankful for?"** If your kids have trouble thinking, ask some questions to help:

- **What are you glad that you have?**
- **What happened that you are happy about?**

Share simple things (jelly for toast, running water, clean socks, etc.), good things that happened, things you learned from the Bible, people who helped you, spiritual blessings, etc.

Read James 1:17. **Every good and perfect gift is from God. God gives blessings—things that bring happiness to His people.**

Do not forget to share your own thankfulness. Teaching kids with words and by modeling thankfulness will help everyone be happier and more content.

108. Let Me Count the Ways

God gives us many *spiritual* blessings. Grab your Bibles and look in Ephesians 1 to see if you can find seven blessings.

Good things God provides for us through Jesus in Ephesians 1:

- Holiness (Ephesians 1:4)
- Family/Adoption (Ephesians 1:5)
- Grace—**G**od's **R**iches **a**t **C**hrist's **E**xpense (Ephesians 1:6)
- Forgiveness of sins (Ephesians 1:7)
- Wisdom (Ephesians 1:8)
- Inheritance (Ephesians 1:11)
- Holy Spirit (Ephesians 1:13)

109. Chasing Wisdom

Run a race with balloons. Make a starting point and a finish line (about 15 feet apart). Give each person a balloon and line up everyone on the starting line. At the signal to go, each one must blow air into his or her balloon and then let it go. Wherever it lands is where he or she must run and do the same thing over and over until one person's balloon crosses the finish line.

Solomon, a very wise man, said that chasing the world's ideas is like chasing the wind (Ecclesiastes 1:17). **If we get what we believe from TV or other people, these beliefs may or may not be right. What are some wrong things others might tell us?** (God does not care what you do. It is okay to tell a lie. Things make you happy. Man evolved from animals, etc.)

We want to be wise so we read and believe God's words in the Bible. We can be sure they are true.

Ask each person to blow up and tie his or her balloon. Then have each person carefully write a Bible truth on the balloon.

Here are a few ideas:

- *God can be trusted (Proverbs 3:5).*
- *God will always love me (Romans 8:39).*
- *God will never leave me (Hebrews 13:5b).*
- *God is powerful (Jeremiah 32:17).*
- *God will do what is best for me (Romans 8:28).*

We must believe these wise Bible truths and not chase after every false idea.

110. One Wish

God appeared to King Solomon (the author of many of the proverbs) in a dream and said, "Ask whatever you want and I will give it to you."

Ask your kids around the dinner table or while driving: *If you could have one wish, what would it be?*

Solomon's one wish was for wisdom—wisdom to rule over the people of Israel. God was so pleased that Solomon had asked for this one thing—the best thing (rather than long life, riches, or his enemies destroyed)—that He gave Solomon wisdom like no one had ever had or will ever have. He also gave Solomon riches, honor, and a long life (1 Kings 3:5-14).

 **The Wisest Thing**

Brainstorm situations where kids will need to make a choice.

Some ideas:

- lost lunch money
- need to do book report, but friend wants you to go to a ballgame
- friends want you to watch a movie your parents have prohibited
- teacher leaves the room and tells class to finish assignment
- you get $25 for your birthday
- you have three hours of free time

After reading each situation, ask: ***What is the wise thing to do?***

Wisdom is defined as not only knowing the right way, but choosing to follow it. It is important to know the wise thing, but it is just as important to DO it.

 **Did They Just Say That?**

While watching movies or TV, be on the lookout for situations and characters that could provide teachable moments.

Ask questions to see what the kids are thinking:

- What do you think of that character's actions? Were they good, bad, or neutral?
- What do you think about the way they handled that situation? What might be a better way to handle that?
- Was his decision a wise one?
- What does the Bible say about that?

Teaching kids wisdom is best done a little at a time.

Quick Reference Guide

Topical Index

Scripture Index

KNOW GOD'S
PURPOSE
FOR YOUR FAMILY
& BUILD
**YOUR LIFE
AROUND IT.**

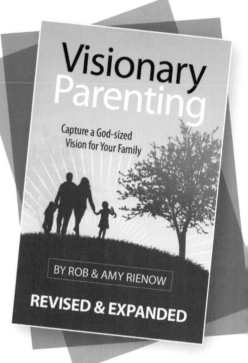

VISIONARY PARENTING
Capture a God-sized Vision for Your Family
by Rob and Amy Rienow

Readers will capture a fresh, God-sized vision for their family. No matter where they are on the parenting journey, they will see God can transform a home. It begins with understanding God's purpose for the family and taking an honest look at the current state of the home. The authors share the foundational truth that God created the family to ensure that each generation grows up to know, love, and serve Him. The Rienows remind readers of the instructions from God given directly to parents in Deuteronomy 6:5-7 that will transform any home.

What is D6®?

BASED ON DEUTERONOMY 6:5-7

A **conference** for your entire **team**

A **curriculum** for every age at **church**

An **experience** for every person in your **home**

Connecting
CHURCH & HOME
These must work together!

D6 CONFERENCE
ONCE A YEAR

DEFINE & REFINE Your Discipleship Plan

www.d6family.com

ONE HOUR
A WEEK

POWER OF
PARENTAL INFLUENCE